doodle!

MOUSTACHES

Over 60 Drawings to Complete & Color

Peter Donahue

Dover Publications. Inc.

Mineola. New York

Embrace your inner hipster with this cool doodle collection. Just grab your crayons, markers, or colored pencils and add an imperial, handlebar, pencil, Fu Manchu, or horseshoe 'stache to 62 fabulous figures ranging from a hippie and a nerd, to ninjas, a gangster, a hip-hop artist, and even a pair of zombies.

Bibliographical Note

What to Doodle? Moustaches: Over 60 Drawings to Complete & Color, first published by Dover Publications, Inc., in 2016, contains a selection of images originally published by Dover in *The Moustache Doodle Book* in 2014.

International Standard Book Number

ISBN-13: 978-0-486-80525-2
ISBN-10: 0-486-80525-5

Manufactured in the United States by RR Donnelley
80525501   2016
www.doverpublications.com

Artist

Magician

Clown

3

Construction guys

5

Hipster I

Hipster II

Motorcycle rider

Selfie

Fireman

Chef

11

Wine snob

12

Waiter

Rock stars

Queen's
guard

Steampunkster

Lunch lady

18

Pilot

Pilgrim

Spartan

Hippie

Lumberjacks

Cowboy

Gunslinger

Snowma

28

Robot?!

29

Gangster

Police
officer

31

Ninjas

Samurai

34

Pharaoh

Mummy

36

Cyclops

38

Zombies

Viking

Tarzan

Pirates

43

Genie

Wizard

45

Mad scientist

Frankenstein monster

Superhero

Leprechaun

49

50   Drill sergeant

Disco stud

51

Oktoberfester

Hip-hop artist

53

54

Sumo wrestlers

55

56

Snowboarder

Surfer

58

Soccer players

Fly fisherman

60

Karate blackbelt

61

Nerd